AMAZING CRIME SCENE SCIENCE

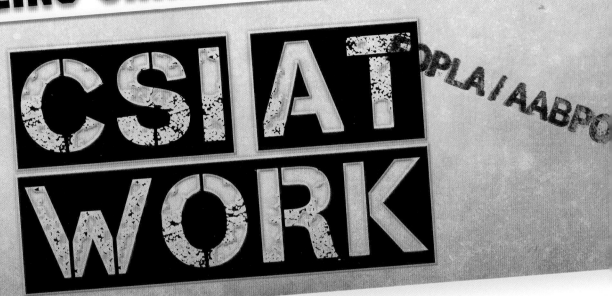

CSI AT WORK

John Townsend

amicus

Published by Amicus
P.O. Box 1329
Mankato, MN 56002

Printed in the United States of America at Corporate Graphics, in North Mankato, Minnesota.

Library of Congress Cataloging-in-Publication Data
Townsend, John, 1955-
  CSI at work / by John Townsend.
     p. cm. -- (Amazing crime scene science)
  Includes bibliographical references and index.
  Summary: "Explores the different steps of crime investigation and the multiple
  methods crime scene investigators use when collecting evidence and solving murders.
  Includes real case files and case studies"--Provided by publisher.
  ISBN 978-1-60753-167-8 (library binding)
  1. Crime scene searches--Juvenile literature. 2. Evidence, Criminal--Juvenile literature.
  3. Criminal investigation--Juvenile literature. 4. Forensic sciences--Juvenile literature. I. Title.
  HV8073.8.T682 2012
  363.25'2--dc22
                             2010033808

Appleseed Editions, Ltd.
Created by Q2AMedia
Editor: Katie Dicker
Art Director: Harleen Mehta
Designer: Neha Kaul
Picture Researchers: Debabrata Sen, Rajeev Parmar

All words in **bold** can be found in the Glossary on pages 30–31.

Picture credits
t=top b=bottom c=center l=left r=right

Brandon Alms/Istockphoto: Title page, c.CBS/Everett/Rex Features: 4, Gustaf Brundin/Istockphoto: 5, Sean Gallup/
Getty Images: 6, Suljo/Istockphoto: 7, Mauro Fermariello/Science Photo Library: 8, Edward Kinsman/
Science Photo Library: 9, Brandon Alms/Istockphoto: 10, Scott Rothstein/Shutterstock: 11, Mauro Fermariello/
Science Photo Library: 12, Corepics/Shutterstock: 13, White/Photolibrary: 14, Corbis/Photolibrary: 15, Sedat Ozkomec/
Rex Features: 16, Eddie Green/Istockphoto: 17, Rex Features: 18, David Zalubowski/AP Photo: 19, Shout/
Rex Features: 20, Mauro Fermariello/Science Photo Library: 21, Alexander Rivosh/Shutterstock: 22, Karam Miri/123RF: 23, Rich
Legg/Istockphoto: 24, Rex Features: 25, Zoubin Zarin/Istockphoto: 26, Lorna/Dreamstime: 27,
Jacob Halaska/Photolibrary: 28, Tonylady/Shutterstock: 29. Eddie Green/Istockphoto: 31.
Cover images: Brandon Alms/Istockphoto, Jan Tyler/Istockphoto, Joan Vicent Cantó Roig/Istockphoto.

DAD0052
3-2011

9 8 7 6 5 4 3 2 1

CONTENTS

Into Action

Soon after the police rush to the scene of a serious crime, they call in experts to examine the area. What goes on behind the scenes where **CSI** (crime scene investigation) officers are at work?

Getting Started

First, the area is made safe and secure. There could be danger, especially if a criminal is hiding, or there may be a risk of fire, explosion, or unsafe materials. The area is roped off to prevent people from entering or touching vital **evidence**. It is also important at this stage that details of the crime remain secret.

This forensic team, on the popular television show *CSI*, arrives at a crime scene.

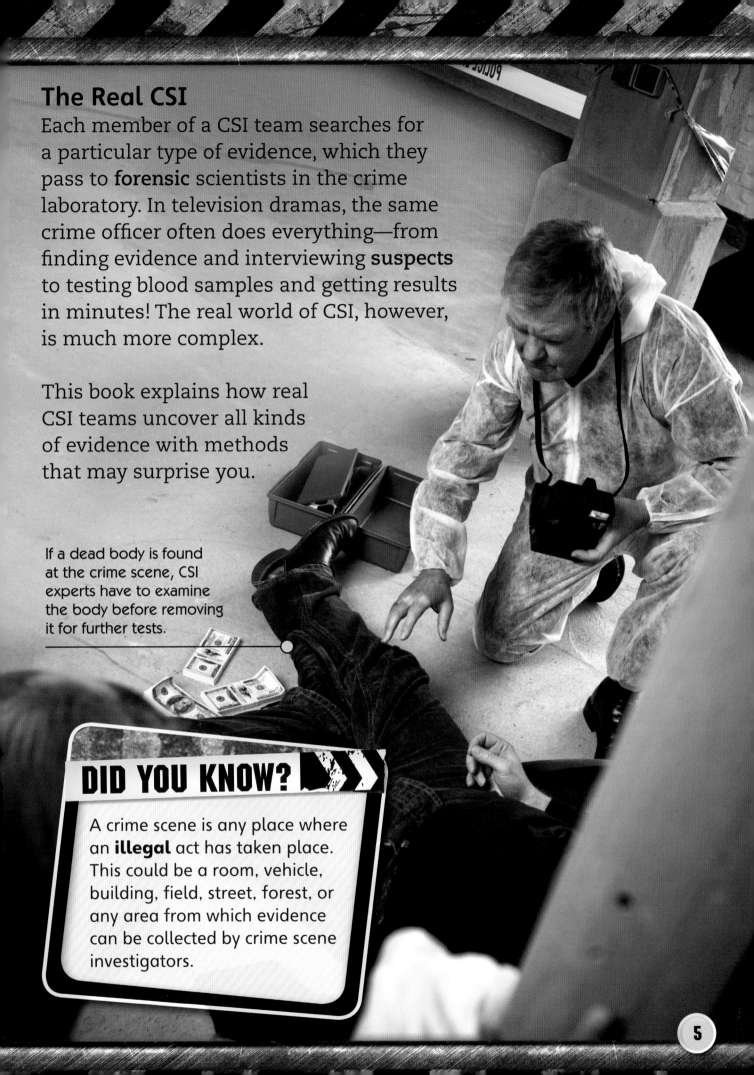

The Real CSI

Each member of a CSI team searches for a particular type of evidence, which they pass to **forensic** scientists in the crime laboratory. In television dramas, the same crime officer often does everything—from finding evidence and interviewing **suspects** to testing blood samples and getting results in minutes! The real world of CSI, however, is much more complex.

This book explains how real CSI teams uncover all kinds of evidence with methods that may surprise you.

If a dead body is found at the crime scene, CSI experts have to examine the body before removing it for further tests.

DID YOU KNOW?

A crime scene is any place where an **illegal** act has taken place. This could be a room, vehicle, building, field, street, forest, or any area from which evidence can be collected by crime scene investigators.

The First Task

After a bank robbery where robbers threatened staff, took money, and ran, the CSI team quickly sets to work at the bank. So what do they do first?

Recording the Scene

Once any witnesses have been helped from the crime scene, the area is taped off and made secure. The task begins of recording every detail of the entire area exactly as the criminals left it. This stage involves photographs, videos, sketches, and detailed notes. Once all the records are complete, the next stage of collecting evidence begins.

CSI officers mark and record evidence found at an attempted bank robbery in Berlin, Germany. Their protective suits prevent contamination of the scene.

The Search for Clues

Crime scene investigators have to find, gather, and preserve all evidence to help answer the key questions at the start of any criminal inquiry:

- What happened exactly and where?
- When did each event occur?
- How many people were involved—and the big question: Who were they?

Any evidence that identifies the criminal must be so reliable that it can be used as proof in **court**.

Evidence that the CSI team might work on includes:

- Impressions (such as fingerprints and tire tracks)
- Hair and fibers
- Body fluids (blood, saliva, and sweat)
- **Trace evidence** (such as gunshot or paint **residue**)
- Weapons evidence (such as knives and guns)
- Documents (such as letters, e-mails, or telephone messages).

A crime scene investigator has tools to take fingerprints, footprints, or blood samples.

Forensic Photography

Taking photographs of a crime scene is a skilled job that involves far more than taking a few quick photos. Proper forensic photographs can actually help to solve a crime.

In the Picture

Before anything is moved, photographs must preserve the crime scene to help the investigation. The position of dead bodies, the shape of bloodstains, and the location of items can be vital to the CSI team's work long after the crime scene has been cleaned up.

A forensic photographer has to act fast to record vital evidence.

Checklist

The photographer will take pictures of:

- The entire area before anyone enters, usually taken from many angles with both wide-angle and close-up shots
- Dead bodies, witnesses, and vehicles nearby
- All major items of evidence in close-up before they are moved, such as a shoe print with a ruler beside it to show its exact size

A forensic photographer often uses numbered markers next to pieces of evidence. These markers help to illustrate written reports. In a murder inquiry, the **victim** may have an **autopsy**—which is also photographed.

New digital photography and software makes it possible to record crime scene information in a single photograph. The image can be shown in 3D as a computer model so the CSI team can study a virtual crime scene.

This special photograph shows the temperature of a dead body. It helps estimate the time of death from light, hot parts to dark, cooler areas.

Spot 19.4 °C

34.1

18.3

Finding Prints

Everyone's fingerprints are **unique**, so they can be matched exactly to individual suspects to prove if they were at a crime scene. Finding this evidence is a key part of CSI work.

Collecting Prints

Using brushes, powders, tape, chemicals, sticky **lift cards**, a magnifying glass, and even super glue, the CSI fingerprint specialist looks for prints on smooth surfaces. These are carefully lifted and sent to a laboratory to identify or rule out a suspect. The three main types of prints are:

- Visible prints: left by the transfer of blood, wet paint, or dirt onto a surface

- Impression prints: left in a soft material such as putty, wax, or soap

- **Latent** prints: left by the transfer of sweat onto a smooth surface but not visible until dusted with special powder

Dusting a weapon with powder helps to reveal invisible fingerprints.

Where and How?

A CSI officer looks for latent prints on surfaces such as around a door or window that was forced open. By shining an **ultraviolet** light onto it, the expert can often uncover latent prints.

Another method was discovered by accident in 1977 by a Japanese forensic scientist. While using super glue to adhere evidence to glass microscope slides, he was amazed to see his own fingerprint develop on the slide's surface. The fumes from the glue caused a chemical reaction with the sweat from his fingers. "Super glue fuming" is still used in many crime laboratories around the world.

A CSI officer transfers a fingerprint onto tape to preserve the print found at a crime scene.

DID YOU KNOW?

Fingerprints must be removed and transported to the crime lab to check them against a database of criminals' fingerprints. Lifting a print is often done with sticky tape or by placing a sticky, clear sheet over dusted prints. A simple method—but the prints are then preserved for future testing.

Tiny Traces

Very small pieces of evidence are usually spread around a crime scene. Fibers, hairs, glass, paint flakes, or tiny blood spots can tell CSI experts a great deal.

Fibers and Hair

Using combs, tweezers, tape, and a filtered suction tool, a CSI specialist collects hair or fibers at the crime scene. Once found, these are sealed in separate containers, labeled, and sent to the laboratory for testing.

Amazingly, the presence of hair on a weapon can link it to a crime. The crime lab can figure out if a hair fell out or was pulled and test it for **DNA** to discover exactly whose hair it is.

Investigators use a suction tool to collect fibers and hair from a car seat. These may be linked to clothing and hair from a suspect.

Blood Traces

If there is dried blood on any furniture at the crime scene, the object is sent to the crime lab. If the blood is on a wall, the CSI blood specialist collects it by scraping blood flakes with a **scalpel** into a sterile container.

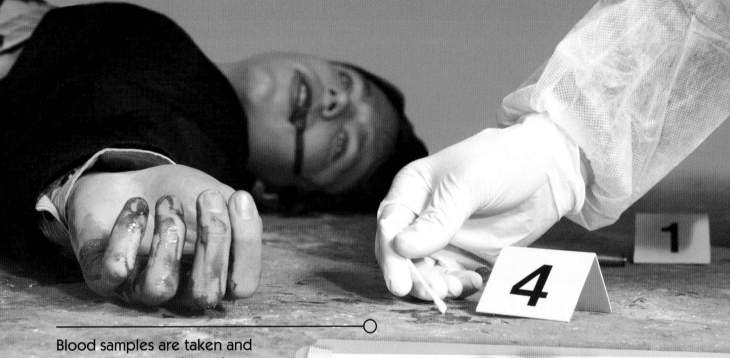

Blood samples are taken and tested for DNA to identify a criminal or a victim.

SCIENCE SECRETS

DNA is a substance in all our blood **cells** (and all our body cells). It can be tested and matched against police records. If there is an exact match to a known criminal, it becomes clear who the **culprit** is. Everyone's DNA is different—except for some identical twins.

CASE FILE

When three women were murdered in four days in 2000 in Birmingham, UK, CSI officers were soon able to trace the murderer, Philip Smith:

- Blood matching each of the three victims was found on Smith's belongings.

- A pink fiber found at Smith's home and car matched fibers from a blanket wrapped around a victim's body.

- Tiny specs of the victims' blood were found on Smith's car.

With all this trace evidence, Philip Smith was sent to prison for life in 2001.

Gun Shots

If criminals fired guns during a crime, there will be various traces of evidence left behind that can give the CSI **ballistics** expert plenty of valuable information.

Bullet Proof

In some crime scenes, the entire area needs to be searched for stray bullets. Depending on where bullets and gunpowder residue are found, the ballistics expert can often determine exactly where a gun was fired. Most guns have their own unique features, such as tiny marks inside the gun barrel that can scratch fired bullets and help identify the gun that was used.

Serial numbers stamped onto some bullets can indicate where they were purchased and sometimes who bought them. Some criminals try to scratch these numbers off their bullets. However, with new scanning technology, it is possible for forensic scientists to find fingerprints on fired bullets.

A CSI officer collects gun evidence at a crime scene, which may hold the link to a killer.

Firearms

When firearms are left at a crime scene, the CSI ballistics expert has to figure out who fired what, where, and when. Bullets and **cartridge** cases may be matched to other crimes.

Bullet holes can reveal the height at which a gun was fired and the position of victims when they were shot. If bullets are embedded in a wall, the CSI team may have to cut out that part of the wall and take it to the laboratory.

A CSI officer measures the bullet hole in a window. Tests may identify glass fragments found on clothing or in wounds.

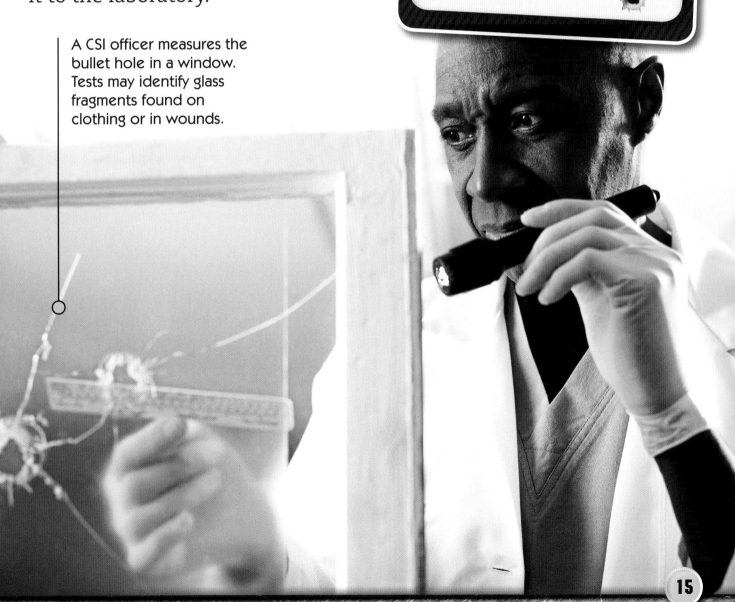

DID YOU KNOW?

CSI ballistics experts sometimes use equipment called a laser **trajectory** kit. This uses laser beams at the crime scene to plot the angles and lines of fire to show where the criminal was standing when the gun was fired.

Crime Tracks

Whether on foot or in a vehicle, criminals often leave tracks somewhere. It is the CSI team's job to find such tracks and use them to help catch the culprits.

Preserving Footprints

No two footprints are exactly the same, and tiny marks on the soles of footwear leave traces behind. Footprints in soil can be photographed, but a CSI specialist often makes a plaster **cast** to preserve the print.

Footprints in snow need to be treated carefully. Sometimes, investigators use liquid **sulfur**, which cools quickly as it touches the snow, to capture the exact impression without damaging it.

CAN YOU BELIEVE IT?

Sometimes, footprints lead immediately to criminals. When thieves raided a shop in Glasgow, Scotland, during a blizzard in 2006, they were caught in minutes with the stolen goods. The police followed them by tracking their footprints through the snow!

A footprint cast taken from a crime scene can be studied in a laboratory.

567627i MUST ... TOS BY: Sedat Ozkomec / Rex Features
THE POLICE FORENSIC LABORATORY, ISTANBUL, TURKEY - 2006 A cast of a footprint

Tire Tracks

Just like footprints, tire tracks can be matched to the exact tire that left the impression. Wear marks on tires and cuts caused by nails or gravel give a unique print. To preserve the track for close study later in the laboratory, a CSI officer pours liquid plaster into the impression. This hardens and is carefully removed, providing a permanent cast of the track on the ground.

Tool Marks

Distinct marks are left when a tool comes into contact with a surface. Criminals often use wire cutters, crowbars, and screwdrivers at crime scenes. These tools leave impressions that investigators can identify and use as evidence when a suspect is eventually arrested.

Tire marks leave a deep impression in sand. These markers have been used to identify gun cartridge cases found at the scene.

On the Wrong Track

Sometimes, tracks and other evidence at a crime scene are missed or ruined. If the entire crime scene becomes contaminated, it is of little further use.

Missing Evidence

The famous murder case of six-year-old JonBenet Ramsey in Colorado has never been solved. Officers were blamed for not treating the crime scene with enough care. Evidence was missed, ruined, and even lost.

At 5:52 A.M. on December 26, 1996, JonBenet's mother called the police. She had found a **ransom** note that her daughter had been kidnapped. The police came by, but at the time, no one knew the house was a murder scene. Important items were touched and moved before any CSI photographs were taken. Friends of the family were allowed to roam around the house.

JonBenet had been murdered in the basement. When her parents eventually found her body, they moved it upstairs, destroying even more evidence.

The case of JonBenet Ramsey is still a mystery.

There was a lot of confusion at the crime scene. It was later said that officers photographed shoe prints in the snow outside the Ramsey home, but this was untrue because most of the snow had melted. A shoe print in the basement could not be used as evidence because so many friends, family, and police had trampled through and disturbed it.

Because it was Christmas, the **pathologist** was away and did not arrive for six hours. By then, it could have been as long as 22 hours since JonBenet died. As such, the exact time of death could never be proved, and vital evidence became useless. The case remains unsolved.

CAN YOU BELIEVE IT?

An autopsy proved that JonBenet had been strangled with a rope. Her skull had also been fractured. She had eaten pineapple only a few hours before the murder, but her mother said there had been no pineapple in the house. However, CSI photographs showed a bowl of pineapple on the kitchen table!

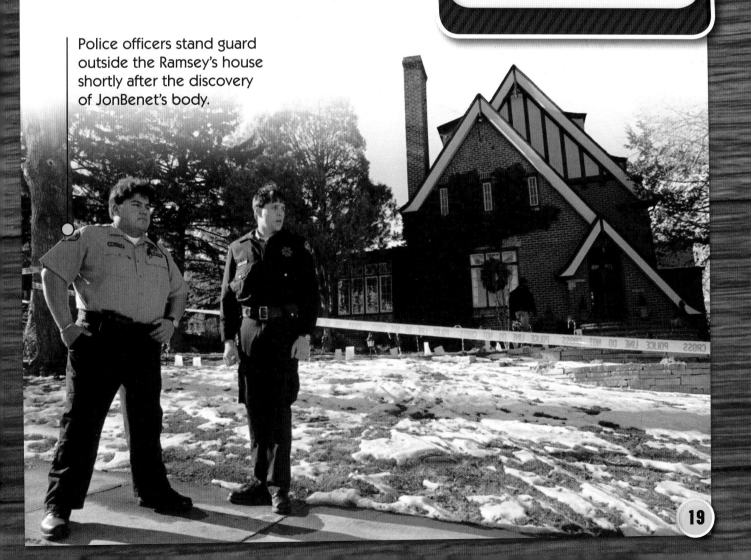

Police officers stand guard outside the Ramsey's house shortly after the discovery of JonBenet's body.

Dog Detectives

One piece of invisible evidence that remains at a crime scene is scent. Who best to track it down than the cold nose of the law—a CSI sniffer dog!

On the Scent

We all leave a trail of skin cells, hair, and sweat, which dogs can detect. Dogs can even tell the difference between recent and older scents. If a criminal walks on a concrete floor and leaves no visible tracks, there are still plenty of invisible signals for a CSI dog to follow.

The nose of a German shepherd dog has about 200 million "smelling cells," which are many times more powerful than a human's nose. This amazing dog super sense not only sniffs out drugs, explosives, and hidden bodies, but also money. Dogs can now be trained to detect different types of bank notes because of the various inks and papers used. How clever is that?

DID YOU KNOW?

Sometimes, CSI teams use a machine that collects smells onto a scent pad. The scent is collected at the crime scene and later given to a dog to sniff. The scent can be freeze-dried and used years later. A trained dog sniffs it and seeks out a suspect.

This bloodhound is being trained to recognize smells found on items of clothing.

Sniffing Out Evidence

If a criminal runs from the crime scene, a tracking dog can soon be on the trail. The CSI dog handler will let the dog sniff an item from the crime scene, such as a piece of clothing, a car seat, or something a suspect left behind. With that scent clearly in its mind, the dog can soon hunt down a hiding culprit.

Crime scene investigators also train some dogs to detect the smell of decaying bodies. Such dogs are vital in murder investigations where a body is missing or hidden. The dogs learn to alert their handlers when they detect the presence of human remains.

Dogs trained to find a dead body are called cadaver (body) dogs. They can even detect the smell of a dead body under water.

K9 Forensics

Crime scene dogs are often called forensic search dogs or just K9 for short—after the word **canine**, which simply means dog.

Missing Woman

In 2001, 36-year-old Kimberly Szumski was reported missing in Philadelphia. She was a fitness instructor and a waitress. She had two young children, but she and her husband Thomas were in the middle of a divorce. When Kimberly strangely disappeared, her car was still in the driveway at the family's home. Thomas appeared very upset and offered a reward if anyone could give information as to the whereabouts of his missing wife.

Friends did not know at the time that Thomas had been in prison for armed robbery and had recently threatened to kill Kimberly. After a big fight with her, Thomas had strangled his wife. He wrapped her body in plastic to make sure she was sealed from any sniffer detective dogs. He then buried her nearby and put large concrete slabs on top of the grave. He built a wall on top of that to make sure the body would remain well hidden.

On the right track— when a crime is difficult to solve, dogs are often the best detectives.

Three months later, CSI officers visited the Szumski house to make further inquiries. They became suspicious and brought in Azeem, a detection dog. Azeem got to work sniffing for clues at a site where Thomas Szumski had recently worked. Amazingly, Azeem picked up the scent of Kimberly's body through the layers of concrete, soil, and plastic. The dog alerted the CSI team, who pulled down the wall to reveal Kimberly's buried body. Azeem had solved the crime!

Trained sniffer dogs can easily tell what is hidden inside bags.

SCIENCE SECRETS

Scientists have studied how a dog's nose works and have even tried to make electronic sniffing devices. Such "e-noses" can recognize some smells, but they are still a long way from being as efficient as a good K9 that can store a "library" of different scents in its brain.

Doubtful Dogs

Using dogs at a crime scene is best when the scent is still fresh. The older the crime scene, the less likely it is that dogs can smell any evidence.

Reliable Methods?

Although dogs can be a great help to CSI teams in their searches, investigations that depend on dogs alone to recognize an object or a person have sometimes been wrong.

Occasionally, the police put a suspect in a scent lineup with other people. A sniffer dog is then brought in to make an identification based on its memory of a scent from the crime scene. However, there have been doubts about the reliability of this kind of "dog evidence."

In a police lineup, witnesses try to identify a suspect from a line of people. Dogs are sometimes used to sniff out a suspect too.

CASE FILE

Madeleine McCann disappeared in 2007 while on vacation with her parents and younger twin brother and sister in Portugal. The British girl was nearly four years old when she went missing from a ground floor apartment while her parents were eating in a restaurant nearby. The story made headline news around the world.

Portuguese police began an investigation, believing Madeleine had either been kidnapped or had died at the crime scene. When a sniffer dog yelped at the apartment, detectives thought this was proof that Madeleine's dead body had been there.

However, the dogs in this case had every reason to be confused. Despite the apartment being a crime scene, different families had stayed there before the McCanns. The sniffer dogs had been trained to smell **corpses** and human blood. They recognized something—but because the scene had been contaminated, nothing could be proved and Madeleine was not found.

Madeleine was almost four years old when she disappeared.

DID YOU KNOW?

A British CSI dog handler said that dogs used to detect a death smell on Madeleine's clothes were brought in too long after she had vanished. This type of scent would last only about a month. Although detectives were unable to piece together what happened on the night that Madeleine disappeared, the hunt for the little girl continues.

Fake Scenes

When is a crime scene not a crime scene?
Sometimes, CSI officers arrive at an incident
that is far from what it seems.

True or False?

What should you do if you come across what you
think is a crime scene? The short answer is to
call the police and try to keep people away until
the professionals arrive. Even if it appears to be
a crime scene, it might not be! Just because a
dead body is slumped on the ground, it might not
mean a crime has taken place. Being able to tell
a genuine crime scene from a deliberate fake can
sometimes be difficult even for the experts.

Is this a murder, a
death from natural
causes, or a fake?

CASE FILE

Linda Anders was murdered at her home in Liverpool, UK, in 2000. A **burglar** attacked her and fled—or so it seemed. Her **disabled** husband told the police he had come home to find his wife's body just as a man pushed him to the ground and ran off.

However, CSI experts found no sign of forced entry. They examined footprints, but none were from the burglar. Then a bloodstain was found on the inside of a shirt worn by Malcolm Anders, the victim's husband. He became a suspect. Malcolm had cleaned up the murder scene and given the impression of a robbery. Malcolm had also faked his disability for years. The **jury** found him guilty of murder, and he was sent to prison for life.

CAN YOU BELIEVE IT?

A high school class on CSI fieldwork studies at Fort Lauderdale, Florida, had a surprise in 2006. The teacher's fake crime scenes with skeletons and bullets had something extra—a dead body. But it was not a fake! A man had died at the scene from natural causes.

Is this a crime scene or just someone's untidy bedroom?

What Next?

Amazing crime scene science continues to develop the accuracy of crime scene investigations. Improving the finding and collecting of quality DNA samples is just one area of progress.

Future DNA

Scientists are now able to identify the **genes** in DNA that give us such things as our hair color. Future DNA samples may be able to reveal not just a suspect's hair color but also their height, race, and possibly the shape of their face from a drop of blood. This is still a long way off, but research continues to improve the information that can be found.

Even so, advanced DNA science will still fail to tell the difference between some identical twins, whose DNA is the same.

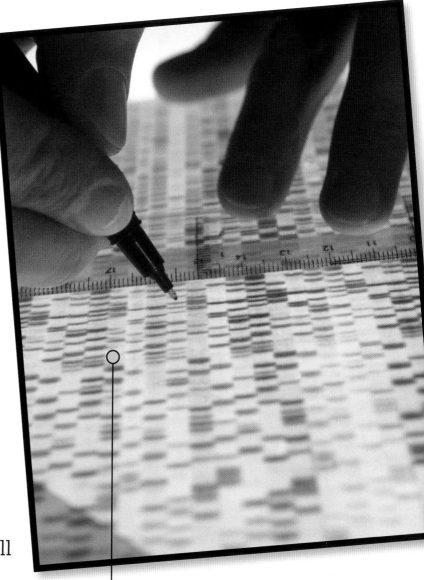

A forensic scientist checks a DNA profile. Comparing profiles from two samples of DNA is called DNA fingerprinting.

CASE FILE

Masked men broke into a Berlin department store in 2009 and stole a fortune in jewelry. CSI officers found traces of DNA on a glove at the crime scene. It seemed one of the thieves would get caught, but the DNA led to *two* suspects—27-year-old identical twins. Forensic scientists were unable to prove which twin committed the crime, and German law only allows criminals to be proven guilty individually.

Even though both men may have committed the crime together, they had to be set free. Forensic scientists also said that the glove could have been placed there by someone else to frame the brothers.

CAN YOU BELIEVE IT?

Even though identical twins share the same DNA, their fingerprints are slightly different. Fingerprint patterns are affected by a baby's position in the **womb** and the growth rate of the fingers. So identical twins will have similar fingerprint patterns, but there will be differences—just as there are tiny differences on each finger on your hand.

Some scientists say they have measured tiny differences in the DNA of certain identical twins. This could make some crimes more solvable in the future.

Glossary

autopsy
an examination of a dead body, especially to find out the cause of death

ballistics
the science of the motion of objects (such as bullets) that are fired

burglar
a criminal who breaks into property to steal things

canine
anything to do with dogs

cartridge
the shell around the gunpowder that fires a bullet

cast
a model made by pouring a liquid, such as plaster, into something so that it hardens into the same shape

cells
the basic building blocks of all living things that are continually renewed

corpse
a dead body

court
the place where a criminal is proven innocent or guilty

CSI
crime scene investigation

culprit
someone guilty of a crime or fault

disabled
when someone is unable to do various tasks due to illness or injury

DNA
the code in each person's cells that makes everyone unique

evidence
material presented to a court in a crime case

forensic
scientific methods to investigate and establish facts in criminal courts

genes
sets of instructions in all our body cells that make us who we are

illegal
anything that is against the law

jury
a group of people in court who must decide whether someone is guilty or not

latent
present but not visible or obvious

lift card
a card used in forensic investigations to store fingerprints that are pressed against its smooth surface

pathologist
a forensic scientist who examines samples of body tissue and dead bodies

ransom
payment demanded for the release of a captured person

residue
waste matter that is left behind after a process

scalpel
a small straight thin-bladed knife

sulfur
a yellow chemical used in making paper, gunpowder, rubber, and molds

suspect
someone thought to be guilty of a crime

trace evidence
small amounts of material such as hair, pollen grains, or soil that can be used as proof in a crime investigation

trajectory
the curve or path that something travels along

ultraviolet
light that can reveal blood and fingerprints that are not visible to the naked eye

unique
only one like it in the world

victim
a person who suffers because of a crime

womb
the space inside a female mammal in which the young develop before birth

Index

Web Finder

www.cyberbee.com/whodunnit/crimescene.html
Solve the crime and be a CSI detective.

http://www.pbs.org/wgbh/nova/sheppard/analyze.html
Solve a mystery that involves creating a DNA fingerprint and comparing this fingerprint to those of the suspects.

www.sciencenewsforkids.org/articles/20060503/Feature1.asp
Learn how scientists use fingerprint evidence to fight crime.

www.sciencenewsforkids.org/articles/20081203/Note2.asp
Find blood at the crime scene, even after the criminal cleans up.